OUR EARTH

Written by
John Malam

Illustrated by
Jim Eldridge, Andrew Harland, Mike Lacey,
Sarah Lees, Gilly Marklew, Dud Moseley,
Sarah Smith, Ross Watton

p

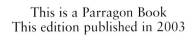

This is a Parragon Book
This edition published in 2003

Parragon
Queen Street House
4 Queen Street
Bath BA1 1HE, UK

Copyright © Parragon 2001

Original book created by

David West ⚧ Children's Books

British Library Cataloguing-in-Publication Data

A catalogue record for this book is available from the British Library.

ISBN 1-40540-277-6

Printed in Dubai,U.A.E

Designers
Aarti Parmar
Rob Shone
Fiona Thorne
Illustrators
John Butler
Jim Eldridge
James Field
Andrew & Angela Harland
Colin Howard
Rob Jakeway
Mike Lacey
Sarah Lees
Gilly Marklew
Dud Moseley
Terry Riley
Sarah Smith
Stephen Sweet
Mike Taylor
Ross Watton
(SGA)
Ian Thompson
Cartoonist
Peter Wilks
(SGA)
Editor
James Pickering
Consultant
Steve Parker

CONTENTS

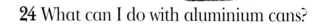

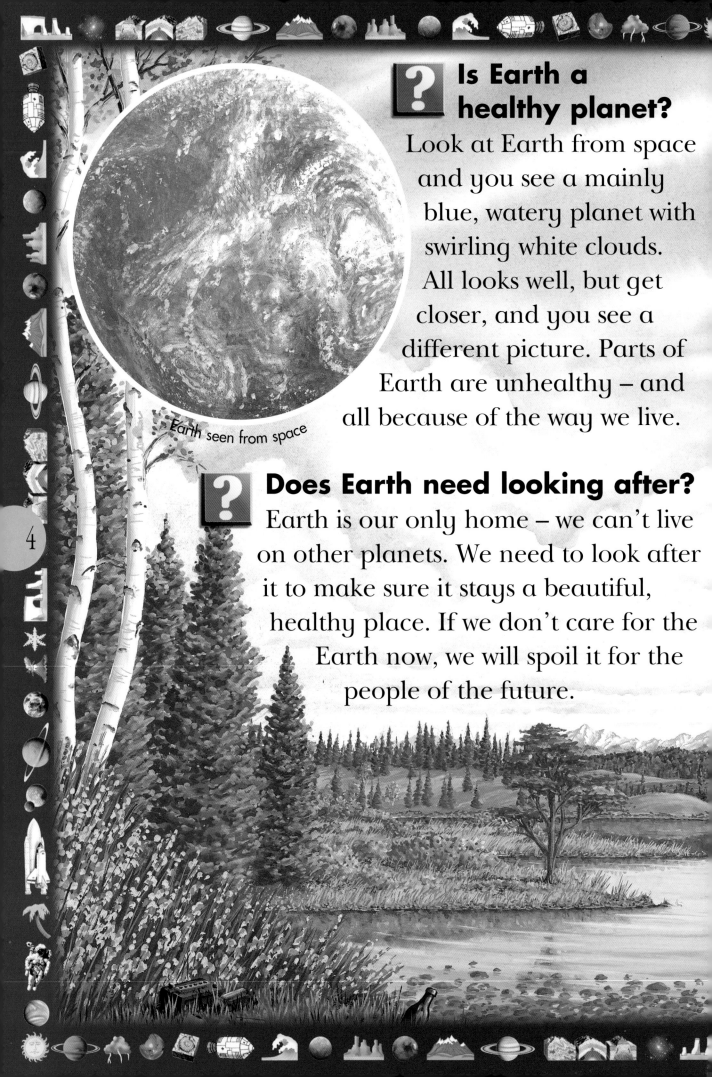

? Is Earth a healthy planet?

Look at Earth from space and you see a mainly blue, watery planet with swirling white clouds. All looks well, but get closer, and you see a different picture. Parts of Earth are unhealthy – and all because of the way we live.

Earth seen from space

? Does Earth need looking after?

Earth is our only home – we can't live on other planets. We need to look after it to make sure it stays a beautiful, healthy place. If we don't care for the Earth now, we will spoil it for the people of the future.

Can I help care for the Earth?

There are many things you can do in your everyday life to care for the Earth. This book tells you about some of them. Just think, if everyone did the same as you, Earth would be a better place to live.

Our Solar System has nine planets which orbit the Sun.

Is it true?
There is no other planet like Earth.

Yes. There is only one Earth. It is special – it is the only planet known to have life on it. Perhaps one day life will be found on another planet, too.

Amazing! There has been life on Earth for approximately 3.5 billion years.

? Is Earth's climate changing?

Earth's climate is slowly getting warmer. Scientists who study the climate have found that it is a little warmer now than it was 100 years ago. You may not notice the difference, but plants and animals do.

Climate study in the Antarctic

Cars and factories burn 'fossil fuels' which produce harmful 'greenhouse gases'.

Is it true?
Trees reduce carbon dioxide in the atmosphere.

Yes. Tree leaves take harmful carbon dioxide from the atmosphere and give out oxygen. We breathe the oxygen they make.

? Why is the temperature rising?

It's getting warmer because of what the Earth's 6 billion people are doing. Because of the way we lead our lives, we are changing the Earth's climate. We are making the planet grow warmer.

Amazing! There is far more carbon dioxide in the atmosphere than there was 200 years ago. This is mainly why it's warmer today than it was in the past.

? How are we making the temperature rise?

By burning 'fossil fuels' – coal, oil and natural gas – we are putting 'greenhouse gases', such as carbon dioxide, into the atmosphere. The gases surround the Earth and keep heat in.

❓ What will happen as the temperature rises?

As the Earth's climate warms up, glaciers and the ice at the North and South Poles will melt, causing the sea level to rise. This will bring floods, and some islands will disappear. Deserts will spread, and droughts will occur.

Amazing! Cows are making the temperature rise. The smelly greenhouse gas methane comes from animals, such as cows, and from factories. Humans make it, too!

How can governments reduce carbon dioxide levels?

Burning petrol in cars puts carbon dioxide into the atmosphere. Governments can build transport systems that don't make carbon dioxide, and order more trees to be planted.

Electric railway

What can I do to help?

Use less electricity. This is because most electricity comes from burning fossil fuels which makes carbon dioxide. Switch off lights, TVs and computers when not in use.

Is it true?
If the Antarctic ice sheet melted, the sea level would rise.

Yes. It holds two-thirds of the Earth's fresh water. If it melted, the sea would rise by up to 70 metres. Coastlines would change all over the world.

Antarctica

What other problems are caused by burning fossil fuels?

Sulphur dioxide is another harmful gas that comes from power stations and vehicles. It is very acidic, which means it eats things away. In the atmosphere, it mixes with droplets of moisture to make acid rain. Trees die when acid rain falls on them and on their soil.

Is it true?
Some polystyrene burger cartons are bad for the Earth's atmosphere.

Yes. Some of them are because they're made using chemicals that damage the ozone layer. Many cartons are now made without these harmful chemicals.

10

Is Earth's atmosphere being harmed?

There is a layer of helpful gas around the Earth called ozone. It protects us from the Sun's dangerous ultraviolet rays. Unfortunately, the ozone layer is damaged because humans have put harmful chemicals into the atmosphere.

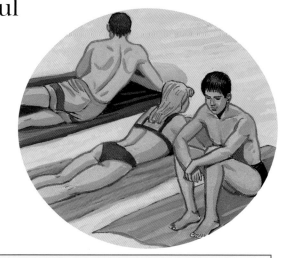

WARNING! Always use a sunscreen in sunny weather to protect your skin from the Sun's rays.

Scandinavian forest damaged by acid rain

 Amazing! When a nuclear power station at Chernobyl, Ukraine, exploded in 1986, radioactive material was sent into the atmosphere. Animals across Europe were contaminated by the radiation.

Underground storage of nuclear waste

Is nuclear power dangerous?

Nuclear power stations do not burn fossil fuels. Therefore, they do not make harmful gases. But they do make radioactive waste material. It is dangerous and will have to be guarded for many years into the future.

❓ Are there alternatives to fossil fuels?

There are other ways to make power. Solar panels collect energy from the Sun. The spinning propellers of wind turbines collect energy from the wind. Each of these energy-collectors makes electricity.

Amazing! Cars can be powered by all sorts of things – solar power, gas, and even chicken droppings!

Wind turbines convert energy from the wind into electricity.

? Are there any other types of natural fuel?

In many countries small amounts of energy come from rotting plants and animal dung. The methane they give off is burned to provide light and heat. This type of fuel is called bio-gas.

Bio-gas plant in India

? Are these fuels better for the Earth?

Yes, they are. Solar power, wind power and bio-gas are cleaner, or 'green', forms of energy. They don't make harmful gases. They don't pollute the atmosphere. They don't make acid rain. They don't harm the ozone layer.

Is it true?
Electricity can be made from water.

Yes. Running water is used to make electricity. This is hydroelectric power. The electricity is made by power stations built in or near dams.

Hoover Dam, USA

13

? Are animals in danger?

Thousands of different animals live on Earth. It is their planet, as well as ours. Sadly, because of what we do, many animals are in danger. An oil spill at sea harms seals, birds and fish. When forests are cut down, many animals lose their homes.

Oil spill

? How many kinds of animals are in danger?

There are many thousands of different kinds of animals in danger. Some are so rare they are endangered. This means they are almost extinct – they have almost died out. If that happens, they will have gone forever.

Endangered species

What is being done to save animals?

Many endangered animals are now protected by law. It is wrong for people to harm them, or the places where they live. Some endangered animals are bred in zoos. This helps to increase their numbers.

Golden lion tamarin

Is it true?
Humans are causing animals to die out.

Amazing! Passenger pigeons used to form flocks of millions of birds, but they were hunted to extinction in the wild. The very last one, named Martha, died in 1914.

Cormorant covered in oil

Yes. It's said that one kind of animal dies out every 30 minutes because of what we're doing to the planet.

15

? Why do people kill certain animals?

Animals are killed for lots of reasons. Birds are killed for their colourful feathers. Elephants are hunted for their ivory. Tigers are killed for their skins. It's against the law, but it still goes on.

Stuffed animals

Amazing! Every year around 100 million animals and plants are taken without permission from the wild. It is because of this that they are endangered.

Collecting rainforest plants

? What about plants?

Like animals, plants can die out too. More than 30,000 different kinds of plants are in danger all over the world. Collectors take them from the wild, or pay local people to do it for them.

Is it true?
Sea turtles are hunted for their shells.

Yes. Even though it's illegal, sea turtle shell, called tortoiseshell, is still used to make spectacle frames and souvenirs for tourists.

? What can I do to help?

Don't buy goods made from ivory, fur, coral or tortoiseshell. Don't pick or dig up wild plants. If you eat tuna fish, make sure it's dolphin-friendly. Dolphins die in some fishing nets.

Illegal animal goods

Why are forests good for the Earth?

Forests are the 'lungs' of the planet. Their trees make much of the oxygen we breathe. Forests provide us with food and timber. Some medicines are made from plants found only in forests.

Rainforest

Are forests in danger?

Forests are in danger in many parts of the world. In some countries trees are killed by acid rain. Elsewhere, whole forests are cut down for their timber, or to make way for farm land.

Logger truck

What is being done to save forests?

Some governments have stopped cutting down the forests on their land. Many forests that are left are protected by law. Also, new forests are being planted, to grow timber like any other crop. It is grown to be cut down.

Amazing! Since 1980, an area of tropical forest six times the size of France has been turned into farm land, or plantations of oil palm, rubber and other crops.

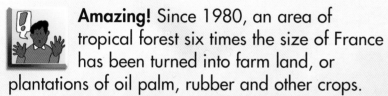

Is it true?
Soil erosion can be seen from space.

Yes. Trees keep soil in place. Where forests are cleared the soil wears away, or erodes, until only rock is left.

Soil erosion on Madagascar, seen from space

How much rubbish do people make?

Too much! People make rubbish and every household makes lots of it every day. In Britain, every family makes about 1.75 kilograms of rubbish each day. Over one year that adds up to more than half a tonne of rubbish!

Is it true?
Some rubbish is dumped at sea.

Yes. Every day thousands of tonnes of rubbish are thrown into the sea. The seabed is littered with rubbish, such as bits of plastic, that never rot away.

Rubbish dump

Rubbish dumped at sea

What happens to all this rubbish?

Because so much rubbish is made, it's a problem to deal with it all. Some is burned inside furnaces. A lot is buried on the land. Some rubbish is collected and sent for recycling.

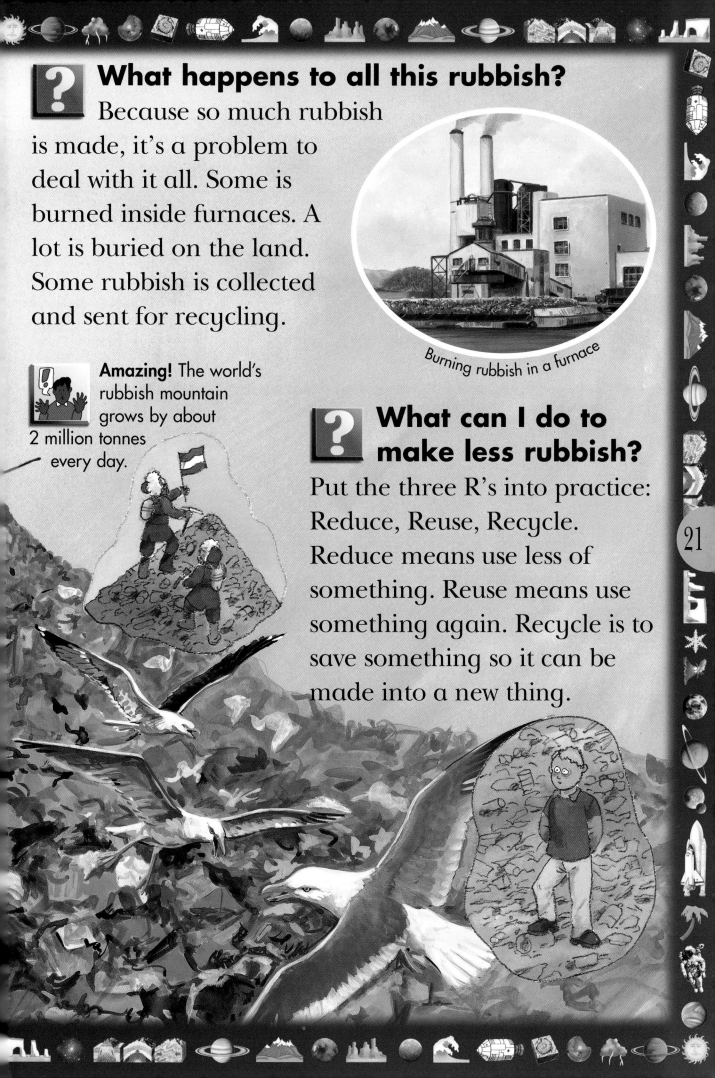

Burning rubbish in a furnace

Amazing! The world's rubbish mountain grows by about 2 million tonnes every day.

What can I do to make less rubbish?

Put the three R's into practice: Reduce, Reuse, Recycle. Reduce means use less of something. Reuse means use something again. Recycle is to save something so it can be made into a new thing.

? What can I do with glass?

When glass bottles and jars are empty, wash them out and take them to a bottle bank. Most supermarkets have bottle banks. When the banks are full, the glass goes to a factory. It is crushed, melted and made into new bottles and jars.

Amazing! Around 6 billion glass bottles and jars are used in Britain every year, but only three out of every ten are recycled.

Bottle bank

What can I do with plastic?

Some kinds of plastic can be recycled. Plastic bottles for fizzy drinks are often made of recyclable plastic. It can be turned into material to make plastic parts for cars. These bottles can also be reused, by making them into useful items.

Reused plastic bottles

Paper recycling

What can I do with paper?

Most paper can be recycled, from newspapers and telephone directories to sweet wrappers and envelopes. It is made into new paper and cardboard.

Is it true?
Glass can be recycled over and over again.

Yes. You just keep on crushing it, melting it and making it into new bottles and jars.

❓ What can I do with aluminium cans?

Cans and tins that hold fizzy drinks and even sardines are often made from a lightweight metal called aluminium. Look for the ALU symbol on them. They can be melted down and made into new cans.

Can recycling

Reusing clothes

Amazing! In Britain we throw away around 11 million aluminium cans every day. If you think that's a lot, the USA throws out 200 million!

What can I do with steel cans?

Using magnets to test cans

Most food cans are made from steel. A magnet will stick to a steel can. If it doesn't stick, the can is probably made from aluminium. Wash the cans out and take them to a can bank. Steel is the world's most recycled material.

What can I do with old clothes?

Give old clothes to charity shops. They are sorted out and many are sold as second-hand clothes. Some old clothes are sent abroad. Tatty clothes are sent to textile mills where they are ripped to pieces and used to make felt.

Is it true?
Christmas trees can be recycled.

Yes. Real Christmas trees (not plastic ones!) can be cut into tiny pieces, called chippings, which are used by gardeners.

❓ What can I do with kitchen and garden waste?

Vegetable peelings, tea leaves and grass cuttings are 'green' waste. If you pile them into a heap in the garden, they will rot down to make compost.

Even some kinds of paper can be turned into compost.

❓ Why is compost good for the environment?

Compost is food for the soil. It contains nutrients (foods) which keep soil healthy. Using home-made compost means less peat compost is dug up from natural places, and animals' homes are saved.

Gardening with compost

❓ Are there other ways of recycling green waste?

You don't need a garden to recycle green waste! You can make small amounts of compost and plant food inside a wormery – a container where a colony of worms live. Worm bins can be kept inside or outside.

Is it true?
Leaves make good compost.

Yes. Leaves rot down slowly to become leaf mould. Put them in a black bag or an open-topped wire cage. After two years you'll have compost.

 Amazing! Green waste in a rubbish tip makes dangerous methane gas, and liquid that can pollute water and kill wildlife. It's safer to make it into compost.

Polluted river

? Are there any dangers to our food?

Some people are worried about genetically modified (GM) foods, where the genes – instructions – have been changed by scientists. Because this has not happened in nature, no one knows how safe these foods are.

Amazing! Pollen from crops that have had their genes changed can mix with organically grown crops. When this happens, an organic crop is no longer organic.

Organic farm of the past

? What does 'organic farming' mean?

It's a natural way of farming where crops are grown and animals raised without using man-made chemicals. Also, the plants and animals have not been changed in any way.

Spraying crops with chemicals can harm the delicate balance of nature.

Is it true?
GM crops need fewer pesticides.

Yes. Scientists are changing the genes inside some crops so that they can resist diseases and pests on their own.

What can I do about it?

It's easy, and fun, to grow some foods at home, such as cress and tomatoes. Be organic, so don't put any chemicals on them. They'll taste good!

Tomato growing

What can I do at home?

Inside the house, start your own recycling centre, collecting materials that can be recycled. Reuse carrier bags, switch off electrical items when they're not in use, and don't leave taps dripping. Outside, get composting, and grow your own organic vegetables.

Amazing! Even an alien would think Earth needs caring for. That's because there are 100,000 pieces of space junk whizzing around the planet.

Energy-efficient house

Insulation to keep the heat in

Switch off electrical items after use.

Don't leave taps dripping.

Cycling is energy-efficient and good exercise.

Grow your own organic vegetables.

Green Club

❓ What can I do at school?

If your school has a Green Club, join it. If it doesn't, ask if one can be started. As at home, switch off lights when they're not in use, and collect paper, cans and glass for recycling. Walk or cycle to school. Try to use cars less.

 Is it true?
You can make a difference.

Yes. Imagine if everyone in your class, your street, even your town recycled things. What a difference that would make!

Sorting rubbish for recycling

❓ How can I find out more?

If you would like to help make the Earth a better, safer place to live, now and in the future, you might like to join groups such as Greenpeace, Friends of the Earth or World Wide Fund for Nature. Your library will have their addresses.

Sort your rubbish for recycling.

Glossary

Acid rain Rain that contains chemicals which are harmful to nature.

Atmosphere The layer of gases around the Earth.

Climate The weather conditions in a particular place on Earth.

Fossil fuels Fuels such as coal, oil and gas, made from fossilised remains.

Genes The instructions that make living things what they are.

Greenhouse gas Gases, such as carbon dioxide or methane, which surround the Earth and keep heat in.

Nuclear power Power made from radioactive material.

Nutrients Chemicals dissolved in water, used by plants in order to grow.

Organic A living thing, or something made from a living thing.

Oxygen A gas that animals breathe in and which keeps them alive.

Peat A dark brown material made from rotten plants.

Radioactive A substance that gives off harmful rays and particles.

Soil erosion Wearing away of the soil.

Solar power Power made from the Sun.

Ultraviolet rays Harmful rays from the Sun.

Index